The Carver Policy Governance Guide Series

*The Policy Governance Model and the Role
of the Board Member*
A Carver Policy Governance Guide, Revised and Updated

Ends and the Ownership
A Carver Policy Governance Guide, Revised and Updated

The Governance of Financial Management
A Carver Policy Governance Guide, Revised and Updated

Adjacent Leadership Roles: CGO and CEO
A Carver Policy Governance Guide, Revised and Updated

Evaluating CEO and Board Performance
A Carver Policy Governance Guide, Revised and Updated

Implementing Policy Governance and Staying on Track
A Carver Policy Governance Guide, Revised and Updated

Praise for the Policy Governance Model

"Reading these guides is a great way to start your journey towards excellence in governance. All the essentials are there, short but clear. And these six guides will also prove to be an excellent GPS device along the way."

 —Jan Maas, PG consultant, Harmelen, The Netherlands

"The guides are a great way to introduce busy board members to the basic principles of Policy Governance. Their bite-size approach is inviting, covering the entire model, albeit in less detail, without over-whelming the reader. They are succinct and easy to read, including practical points of application for board members. Consultants asked to recommend initial reading about the model can do no better than these guides."

 —Jannice Moore, president, The Governance Coach™,
 Calgary, Canada

"Boards introduced to Policy Governance quickly become hungry for information but are short on time. These guides help board members quickly absorb the key principles of the Policy Governance model. They are invaluable."

 —Sandy Brinsdon, governance consultant,
 Christchurch, New Zealand

"For some board leaders the governance elephant is best eaten one bite at a time. The Carver Policy Governance Guide series provides a well-seasoned morsel of understanding in a portion that is easily digested."

 —Phil Graybeal, Ed.D., Graybeal and Associates, LLC,
 Greer, South Carolina

"Would you or your board benefit from a quick overview of essential governance concepts from the world's foremost experts on the topic, John and Miriam Carver? Thanks to their new six-booklet series, you can quickly familiarize or refresh yourself with the principles that make Policy Governance the most effective system of governance in existence. These booklets are the perfect solution for board members who are pressed for time but are dedicated to enhancing their own governance skills."

 —Dr. Brian L. Carpenter, CEO, National Charter
 Schools Institute, United States

The Governance
of
FINANCIAL
MANAGEMENT

Revised and Updated

JOHN CARVER
MIRIAM CARVER

JOSSEY-BASS
A Wiley Imprint
www.josseybass.com

Published by Jossey-Bass
A Wiley Imprint
989 Market Street, San Francisco, CA 94103-1741   www.josseybass.com

Library of Congress Cataloging-in-Publication Data

Carver, John.
  The governance of financial management: a Carver policy governance guide / John Carver and Miriam Carver.—Rev. and updated ed.
    p. cm.—(The Carver policy governance guide series)
  ISBN 978-0-470-39254-6 (alk. paper)
  1. Directors of corporations. 2. Corporate governance. I. Carver, Miriam Mayhew. II. Title.
HD2745.G68 2009
658.15—dc22

2009003151

REVISED AND UPDATED EDITION
HB Printing   10 9 8 7 6 5 4 3 2 1

All boards worry about money. They should. After all, they are accountable for how their organizations handle money. But the board is accountable for everything, not just money. Therefore, in this Guide, our description of governing financial matters is based on broader principles, ones that describe the whole job of the board, not just one part of it.

The Carver Policy Governance Guide titled *The Policy Governance Model and the Role of the Board Member* contains a full description of the Policy Governance model, an operating system for boards. But in case you haven't read it, we start this Guide with a brief overview of this powerful but different approach to the job of the board.

Policy Governance in a Nutshell

- The board exists to act as the informed voice and agent of the owners, whether they are owners in a legal or moral sense. All owners are stakeholders but not all stakeholders are owners, only those whose position in relation to an organization is equivalent to the position of shareholders in a for-profit corporation.

- The board is accountable to owners that the organization is successful. As such, it is not advisory to staff but an active link in the chain of command. All authority in the staff organization and in components of the board flows from the board.

- The authority of the board is held and used as a body. The board speaks with one voice in that instructions are expressed by the board as a whole. Individual board members have no authority to instruct staff.

- The board defines in writing its expectations about the intended effects to be produced, the intended recipients of those effects, and the intended worth (cost-benefit or priority) of the effects. These are *Ends policies*. All decisions made about effects, recipients, and worth are *ends* decisions. All decisions about issues that do not fit the definition of ends are *means* decisions. Hence in Policy Governance, means are simply not ends.

- The board defines in writing the job results, practices, delegation style, and discipline that make up its own job. These are board means decisions, categorized as *Governance Process policies* and *Board-Management Delegation policies*.

- The board defines in writing its expectations about the means of the operational organization. However, rather than prescribing board-chosen means—which would enable the CEO to escape accountability for attaining ends—these policies define limits on operational means, thereby placing boundaries on the authority granted to the CEO. In effect, the board describes those means that would be unacceptable even if they were to work. These are *Executive Limitations policies*.

- The board decides its policies in each category first at the broadest, most inclusive level. It further defines each policy in descending levels of detail until reaching the level of detail at which it is willing to accept any reasonable interpretation by the applicable delegatee of its words thus far. Ends, Executive Limitations, Governance Process, and Board-Management Delegation policies are exhaustive in that they establish control over the entire organization, both board and staff. They replace, at the board level, more traditional documents such as mission statements, strategic plans, and budgets.

- The identification of any delegatee must be unambiguous as to authority and responsibility. No subparts of the board, such as committees or officers, can be given jobs that interfere with, duplicate, or obscure the job given to the CEO.

- More detailed decisions about ends and operational means are delegated to the CEO if there is one. If there is no CEO, the board must delegate to two or more delegatees, avoiding overlapping expectations or causing disclarity about the authority of the various managers. In the case of board means, delegation is to the CGO unless part of the delegation is explicitly directed elsewhere, for example, to a committee. The delegatee has the right to use any reasonable interpretation of the applicable board policies.

- The board must monitor organizational performance against previously stated Ends policies and Executive Limitations policies. Monitoring is only for the purpose of discovering if the organization achieved a reasonable interpretation of these board policies. The board must therefore judge the CEO's interpretation, rationale for its reasonableness, and the data demonstrating the accomplishment of the interpretation. The ongoing monitoring of the board's Ends and Executive Limitations policies constitutes the CEO's performance evaluation.

Figure 1 demonstrates many of these points. The circle represents every possible decision and actual performance of the entire organization, including the board. You can see that the board has made the broadest policies about every policy category, in sufficient

Figure 1. The Policy Circle.

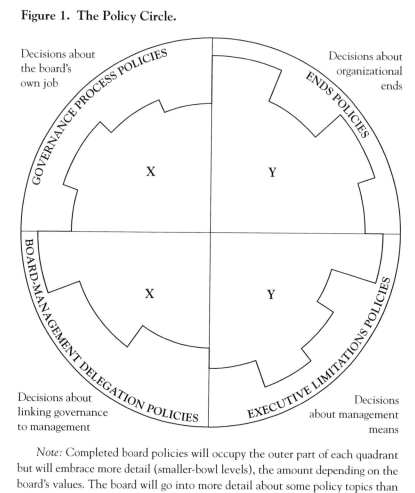

Decisions about the board's own job

Decisions about organizational ends

GOVERNANCE PROCESS POLICIES

ENDS POLICIES

X   Y

BOARD-MANAGEMENT DELEGATION POLICIES

EXECUTIVE LIMITATIONS POLICIES

X   Y

Decisions about linking governance to management

Decisions about management means

Note: Completed board policies will occupy the outer part of each quadrant but will embrace more detail (smaller-bowl levels), the amount depending on the board's values. The board will go into more detail about some policy topics than others, even within a given quadrant. Notice that the quadrant containing all staff means issues will be addressed by the board in a constraining or negative fashion (hence the policy category titled "executive limitations"). Empty space in the middle represents smaller decisions that the board is content to leave to delegatees. The CGO will be given authority to make decisions in the spaces marked X. (Foreshadowing later discussion of this role, CGO is used to indicate the chief governance officer, a function normally fulfilled by the board chair.) The CEO will be given authority to make decisions in the space marked Y.

depth to allow either the CEO (right side) or the CGO (left side) to use and achieve any reasonable interpretation of those policies. You can see that both the CEO and the CGO work for the board and that neither works for the other. You see that both are empowered to make decisions but in strictly different domains.

We include the circle diagram to help you visualize the nature of board control. You can see that the board has made a policy about everything, but none of the policies go into every detail about everything. This is as true of its policies about financial management as about anything else.

Governing Financial Issues

We have frequently found that board members new to Policy Governance mistakenly assume that financial matters are addressed by Ends policies. The ends concept includes a "worth" element, in terms of cost or priority. Since the ends concept may include a "cost" element, isn't anything that relates to costs governed by Ends policies?

No, because "cost" in ends addresses total cost for results, not component costs or the management of finances. For example, for a school system, the cost of the ability to read at a seventh-grade level versus a sixth-grade level is the kind of cost that is in fact an ends issue (though not necessarily one the board chooses to control directly). However, the costs of teachers' salaries, building heating, or insurance are not ends issues. Just because cost is involved offers no clue to whether it is an ends issue or means issue; you must consider what it is a cost *of*. Moreover, priorities are treated the same way; that is, priorities among results or recipients is an ends issue, but priorities among various ways of operating are not. We cannot overstress how critical it is in Policy Governance to apply the definitions of ends and means meticulously. Until that differentiation becomes second nature, it is imperative that any board discussion of an issue begin by strictly determining whether the issue is one of ends or means.

With few exceptions, the subject matter normally referred to as financial management is not one of ends but operational means. Let's list a few of those exceptions so we can put them aside and deal with the board's control over operational finances. In organizations incorporated under for-profit statutes, ends are usually stated in terms of the financial return on shareholders' investment—the familiar term is *shareholder value*. In some cooperative organizations, dividends or patronage payable to members are ends issues. In some fundraising organizations that transfer money to other organizations, that money delivered to other organizations is an ends issue. In other words, only when the organization exists, at least in part, so that some recipient group receives money can that feature of finance be considered an ends issue.

For all other organizations—and for that matter, even for the foregoing organizations' handling of all other financial matters—financial decisions are operational means. We know that they are means because they do not designate any one of the three elements of the ends concept. To put a finer point on it, with the exception just noted, nothing in an income statement or balance sheet designates the recipient result, the recipients, or the worth of such results. As operational means, any board control to be exercised will be done through the use of Executive Limitations policies.

So if you are a board member, we understand that for good reason financial matters can be daunting. But failing to stick with a sound oversight system because finances seem so unlike other issues is like ignoring your plane's instruments just when you need them the most.

"But," you may be thinking, "financial management is really important!" True. However, the ends-means distinction is not based on importance. Both ends and means are important, so you can't tell them apart that way. "But there are legal or contractual requirements regarding some aspects of financial management," you may be thinking. Also true. But because something is legally required does not make it an ends issue. "But financial decision making has the fearsome ability to destroy the organization's ability to produce ends or even destroy the organization itself." Yes, and that is why board control of worrisome aspects of financial management is so important. But being terrifying is not part of the ends definition.

Policy Governance does not downplay the importance of board control of financial management. In fact, Policy Governance calls for more studied, more focused, more demanding control. Responsible governance with respect to finances is not achieved by hours of minute inspection of budgets and financial reports; it is achieved by a board's becoming very clear what constitutes jeopardy, then putting in place a mechanism to prevent it or, should it occur, to discover it as soon as possible.

Fortunately, as you may have noticed, the Executive Limitations approach to controlling means does not require that board members have extensive subject matter skills in the area controlled. This is quite different from the assumptions made by non–Policy Governance boards that board members, or at least some of them, must have extensive financial management skills. Board members using the Executive Limitations approach may certainly need advice and help. They can get that from other board members, auditors, or other independent experts, but they do not themselves need to be finance wizards.

What they do need to know are sources of risk and indicators of financial jeopardy. There are enough financial data points to completely overwhelm. But by focusing on the consequential few, boards need not be awash in and bewildered by the inconsequential many.

Governing Finances with Board Approvals

You have noticed that boards tend to spend a great deal of time poring over numbers. They do so, we assume, because they are aware that the organizations they govern can get into serious trouble quickly if money is mishandled. They want to be sure that it wasn't. We applaud the intent of this painstaking scrutiny. But we point out that no matter how carefully reports are studied, there is no way of finding whether the organization has ventured into what the board deems unacceptable territory if "unacceptable" has not been defined. Of course, an individual board member may be able to find actions, amounts, ratios, or other measures that he or she finds unacceptable. Further, the board can tally these opinions to arrive at whether some financial decision or performance crosses the previously undefined line. These steps can be taken and, in fact, describe the typical board approval process.

But that typical process has two troublesome weaknesses. First, because the board produces these criteria "on the fly," the CEO must guess beforehand what they will be. The effect is more to unearth errors than to inform the CEO what is to be heeded so it can be included in financial management to begin with. Second, this kind of inspection is weakened when a board member with a penchant for finding certain mistakes or favorite concerns is not in attendance for the relevant meeting. The effect in this case is that a happenstance of attendance changes the criteria. The approval process, then, rarely actually sets criteria so much as it identifies one or more specifics unacceptable to various board members. That kind of knowledge is a spotty way to inform the CEO of the criteria or range of latitude the board will accept next time or, indeed, exactly what it was even this time.

Thus it is that the approval method used by traditional boards, however well intended, has only modest effect as a real control over unacceptable financial decisions, actions, and circumstances. It violates the elementary rule that the first step in getting matters to turn out the way you want is to say clearly, specifically, and authoritatively what you want. In other words, a board should say what it wants or wants avoided instead of skipping that step and then judging whether it likes what it gets.

We picture the traditional approval method working like this: the CEO and staff produce reports describing, commonly, what has already taken place. Because of law, regulation, or tradition, the reports are taken to the board for its approval. The board is confronted with levels of detail far beyond its need to know and perhaps its ability to understand. Asked to indicate that the material has nonetheless been found acceptable (approved), the board finds itself in a dilemma. To approve material just because it is there is rubber-stamping, which boards understandably are reluctant to engage in. To prevent rubber-stamping from occurring requires questioning about the very details the board may not have needed to know in the first place.

Many call this micromanaging, although we have observed that the definition of the terms *rubber-stamping* and *micromanaging* seems to depend on who is doing the defining. To be sure, some of the questions asked during an approval process focus on important aspects that the board may want to control. But why should the board wait until the meeting in question to emphasize the aspect (if, indeed, it is the board emphasizing it, not just a board member)? In effect, the CEO is trying to please—or get the approval of—a series of individuals rather than simply demonstrate compliance with policies expressed by the board as a whole. In Policy Governance,

> So if you are a board member and parent, you know you can announce your kid's room to be a mess with no further guidance or you can tell him or her what you expect it to look like, then later judge on that only. The result is better as well as being perceived as fairer.

individual board members' opinions still matter, but they matter as part of the board's deliberation in choosing criteria to begin with. They do not matter in the sense of imposing individual expectations on the CEO in addition to the board's official ones.

Our comments about the problems associated with the usual board approval method apply to all financial approvals, including those of budgets, financial statements, investment reports, and other financial matters. Of course, they apply in exactly the same manner to board approvals of nonfinancial matters. When criteria have been adequately set for subordinates' performance, demonstration of compliance is certainly needed, but there is no need for approval. Consequently, we can say that approving things in the usual sense does not show that a board is doing its job but that a board has *not* done its job.

Governing Financial Issues with Executive Limitations

The Policy Governance board knows that while not all means can be justified by the ends, most can be. And some cannot be, not because they may not work but because they are imprudent (including unlawful) or unethical. The board starts its Executive Limitations policies by stating at the very broadest level its definition of unauthorized operational means. Below this overarching policy starting point, most financial Executive Limitations policies are further definitions of the word *imprudent*. We will examine some often used examples of financial Executive Limitations policies in this Guide and explain their various elements.

So if you are a board member without financial skills, don't try to be a quick-study accountant. Learn what kinds of financial activity or situations jeopardize your organization's integrity or future. Calculating, say, liquidity requires accounting; deciding how much risk is too much requires intelligent consideration. The latter is your job; the former doesn't have to be.

At this point, however, we will point out that when the board deliberates its values about prudence, taking whatever input it needs to examine and clarify those values, it will decide not what decisions and actions should occur but what decisions and actions should *not* occur. (The rationale for this negative or limiting format is explained in the Carver Policy Governance Guide titled *The Policy Governance Model and the Role of the Board Member*.) Policies tend to be rather short when this approach is taken. Boards quickly learn that there are many, perhaps an infinite number, of ways that finances can be managed that are acceptable but that there are only a few ways that are not acceptable. It is the few that are not acceptable that the board must define, and the board needs to know that its relatively small number of carefully chosen controls is respected. Monitoring board policies (which we discuss in detail in the Carver Policy Governance Guide titled *Evaluating CEO and Board Performance*) requires not countless details reported unrelated to any criteria, but a few important data presented in the context of board-established criteria.

When we speak of financial management, we are referring chiefly to four major facets of that topic, ones leading to the policy titles used by many Policy Governance boards. These policy topics are actual financial condition and activities, planned financial condition and activities (budget), asset protection, and investment management. For boards not operating in the Policy Governance framework, the budget is the most recognized, most discussed, and most agonized-over of the four topics. In Policy Governance, a board will normally create a policy specific to each of the four but does not emphasize budget over the others. Later in this Guide, we show examples of financial policies that our clients have written under these four headings. We do not imply, however, that these examples would be acceptable to all boards, for the actual policy content might differ due to circumstances. But the examples will give you an idea of what policies governing financial matters look like.

Policy Control of Actual Financial Condition and Activities

Board members typically encounter the word *actual* used to refer to a report on what has really happened to date with each of the many categories or lines previously budgeted. *Actual* is how it really is, while *budget* is how it was planned to be. Typically, boards put a great deal more attention on budget than on actual. Yet if the board were for some reason allowed to worry about only one of the two, it should definitely worry about actual rather than budget. Budgets may aim an organization toward problems or fail to avoid the risk of problems, but when they become real problems, their status is in actual. Going broke, for example, is a matter of actual.

So we will start our examination of financial Executive Limitations policies by looking at the issues we have found boards want to control about ongoing actual financial condition and activities. What in the myriad features of financial matters does the board want the organization to avoid? If this is definable, Executive Limitations board policy is well on its way to being written.

Let us assume the very largest Executive Limitations policy has already been written. As we explain in the Carver Policy Governance Guide titled *The Policy Governance Model and the Role of the Board Member*, that policy would have prohibited the CEO from allowing actions, decisions, and situations that are imprudent or unethical. (The wording may differ, but the global reach is our point.) This broad policy itself covers a board's worries about financial management, but the breadth of the interpretation of words at this level is rarely acceptable to a board. That is, it must go into greater detail about various areas of some or all operational means; in this case, we are concerned only with the financial ones. As the board further defines its words by going to the next level of policy, it finds two major classes of imprudence.

First, boards know it is possible for good financial management to result in financial viability but not effectiveness. For example, an organization can make financial decisions without regard to the ends it is expected to accomplish but nonetheless be financially healthy. Think of a nonprofit organization for which there is no evidence that intended beneficiaries have the intended impacts in their lives but which is operating in the black, and you have an example of this condition.

Second, boards know that financial management can be conducted in a manner that threatens financial viability. They would find this situation unacceptable even if ends are being accomplished, for that accomplishment may not be sustainable in the long term. Think of a nonprofit organization for which there is evidence that intended beneficiaries do have the intended impacts in their lives but which is running itself into the ground financially or taking improper risks, and you have an example of this condition.

These two classes of imprudence usually form the broadest level of the board's policy about actual financial condition and activities. This policy begins at the second level of specificity after the first all-inclusive or global level. We show an example of this language below. It is important to remember that preceding this more specific policy would be a global Executive Limitations policy very broadly prohibiting unethical or imprudent decisions, activities, and circumstances.

> *Policy Category:* Executive Limitations
>
> *Policy Title:* Actual Financial Condition and Activities
> With respect to the actual ongoing financial condition and activities, the CEO shall not cause or allow the development of financial jeopardy or a material deviation of actual expenditure from board priorities established in Ends policies.

Having settled the content of this policy level, the board must consider whether it will allow the CEO to use any reasonable interpretation of this language. Most boards will not, preferring to establish tighter control over what the definition of financial jeopardy must include. Common further interpretations made by the board of the term *financial jeopardy* include the control of expenses as a percentage of revenues or assets. Hence at the next level, the board might establish a policy provision that would state that the CEO

> . . . "shall not expend more funds in the year to date than have been received in the year to date."

or alternatively, perhaps for a credit union or similar organization,

> . . . "shall not allow expenditures in the fiscal year to exceed 9 percent of total assets."

Boards may if they choose decide to hold assets to which the CEO has no access. In such a case, the board would deny the CEO the right to

> . . . use any long-term reserves. (If this restriction is imposed, it follows that the safety and return of long-term reserves must be added to the board's job, for if it is not the CEO's job, it must be the board's.)

It is usual for boards to want to control the amount of indebtedness that can be incurred; therefore, a further policy provision could be that the CEO

> . . . "will not incur debt in an amount greater than can be repaid by certain, unencumbered revenue within sixty days."

Since boards are aware that these criteria can be met by the simple expedient of withholding the settlement of payables, they often add that the CEO

> . . . "shall not settle payroll and other payables in an untimely manner"

and

> . . . "shall not allow tax payments and other government ordered payments or filings to be overdue or inaccurately filed."

Further, a board may fear that political or other considerations may inhibit the collection of receivables and add that the CEO

> . . . "may not allow receivables to go unpursued after a reasonable grace period."

Although it is unusual for a board to add more detail to the policy than is shown here, each board has the right both to add more items and to take single items into more detail. But the board should only expand its policy if it is not prepared to accept any reasonable interpretation of what it had said in the policy already.

We will not closely examine the monitoring of this and other board policies in this Guide; the Carver Policy Governance Guide titled *Evaluating CEO and Board Performance* is dedicated to the topic of evaluating performance. We do, however, point out that monitoring in the Policy Governance system is always against board-stated criteria, and policies such as those shown above are the criteria. Many of the provisions of this policy require data that are either not found or are hard to find in a traditional financial report. This is why we state that management documents make poor monitoring tools for the board and that the board should expect reports tailored to its policies. The standard financial reports work well for management, but they are a distraction from good governance in the boardroom. They contain possibly hundreds of answers to questions not actually asked while obscuring or completely omitting answers the board needs to know.

Policy Control of Financial Planning or Budgeting

With an Executive Limitations policy like the foregoing sample, the board will have addressed its great fear about deteriorating financial viability, whether caused by poor planning or unexpected circumstances. Let us now turn to the board's concern about budgeting. Budgeting or financial planning is an important managerial process meant, among other things, to ensure that subsequent financial actual comes out right.

It is a time-honored habit for boards to examine budgets, sometimes line by line, prior to approving them, an action that in Policy Governance is unnecessary and dysfunctional. Yet it is also true that no amount of care prevents a budget from needing adjustment repeatedly during the fiscal year. That many of the numbers in the budget will need to be changed tells us that the important features of the budget are not the exact numbers themselves but the principles and values by which staff constructs a budget or a board judges it. Having already made the overarching policy prohibiting decisions, actions, and conditions that are unethical and imprudent, the board in Policy Governance must then reflect on what would make a budget unapprovable if it were subjected to the approval process.

You can make a case that with Ends policies specifying the organizational product and with an Executive Limitations policy putting boundaries on the ongoing actual financial condition, there is no need for the board to address budget at all, even by policy. In other words, if the other policies are fulfilled, budgeting must have succeeded in its part of the job, so there is no discrete need to control it. Despite that consideration, most boards' fear of financial peril is so great that they want the perceived further safety of controlling financial planning anyway.

So what are the limitations that boards typically want to put on budgeting? Upon reflection, boards commonly find that they'd be disturbed by budgeting that bears no discernible relationship to priorities established in their Ends policies. Further, since budgets are normally one-year plans, it would be shortsighted if the one year does not flow from considerations of a multiyear period. And perhaps most obvious of all, a budget that in effect plans to make financially unsound decisions is almost as imprudent as actually making them. Hence the boards will often begin their policy on budgeting as follows. Once again, we emphasize that what we show here are examples of policy provisions; while the method can work for all boards, we do not imply that these examples would be acceptable to all boards.

> *Policy Category:* Executive Limitations
>
> *Policy Title:* Financial Planning (Budgeting)
>
> The CEO shall not cause or allow financial planning for any fiscal year or the remaining part of any fiscal year to deviate materially from the board's ends priorities, risk financial jeopardy, or fail to be derived from a multiyear plan.

Having settled the content of this policy level, the board must consider whether it will allow the CEO to use any reasonable interpretation of the language of the policy. If it will not, it must further define its terms.

When boards consider the interpretation of the term *financial jeopardy*, they see that they may have already defined it in the policy about actual financial condition and activity. There is little point in defining it again, so most boards find it useful to state that they do not authorize the CEO to allow budgeting to

> . . . "risk incurring those situations or conditions described as unacceptable in board policy on financial condition and activities."

Many boards recognize that budgeting is imprudent if the assumptions underlying the projected numbers are unreliable or inadequately conservative, so they might add to the policy that the CEO

> . . . "shall not omit credible projections of revenues and expenses, separation of capital and operational items, cash flow, and the disclosure of planning assumptions."

At this point, the only item left for many boards to concern themselves with is that the CEO reserve or put aside some funds for the board to use for its governance job. Board decisions about costs of governance the organization will bear are recorded in the Governance Process section of policies. To tie the board's intent to CEO action, the Executive Limitations policy about budget might forbid the CEO to

> . . . "provide less for board prerogatives during the year than is set forth in the Cost of Governance policy."

You have of course noticed that this policy has little to say about the numbers in the budget and focuses directly on the prudence with which planning is carried out. Although the CEO might use actual numbers excerpted from a budget to prove the degree of prudence required by reasonable interpretations of the policy, the board's intent is to settle its concern about financial prudence, not specific numbers.

Perhaps you are wondering what to do with a possible conflict between the principles of Policy Governance and the requirements of funders or regulators with respect to budget approval. Many boards of nonprofit and governmental organizations are required to approve budgets and sometimes other documents too. If this is the case, Policy Governance boards use a special "required approvals agenda" in which material that the board is required to approve is presented to the board by the CEO along with evidence that the documents are in compliance with applicable board policies. If the documents in fact are in compliance with applicable board documents, there would be no reason for the board not to approve them. This special agenda is dealt with, therefore, by consent and is quickly dispensed with. This consent approval, it can be argued, is more meaningful than the funder or regulator required. The outside authority wants an approval and rarely, if ever, requires that the approval be based on carefully considered, board-specified criteria.

In some organizations, such as city government and public school systems, budgets are open to community inspection and consultation. We urge the boards of such governments to hold planning meetings with the public as a routine part of their work, taking the opportunity to focus on ends. If such frequent and weighty consultations are held and participation is actively solicited, the detailed planning can be done by the CEO based on the board's decisions that are based on owner (in these cases, public) input of the most crucial kind.

Policy Control of Asset Protection

Beyond the issues of actual financial condition and of financial planning, it would be unwise for boards to overlook their opportunity to control the protection of the organization's assets. The consequences of a failure to protect assets would be a reduction or loss of organizational viability and a consequent inability to produce ends. However, with the global Executive Limitations policy in place prohibiting imprudence, we must first recognize that at this broad level (albeit perhaps unacceptably broad), asset protection has already been mandated.

Therefore, because the global Executive Limitations policy is usually thought far too broad (that is, open to too large a range of CEO interpretation), we now turn to the next Executive Limitations policy used to impose further control over the protection of assets. Just as a board can increase control over actual financial condition and budgeting by taking its policymaking into more depth, it can do the same with asset protection.

We are using the term *assets* here in a very general sense. The sample below goes beyond including buildings, computers, and funds to also include public image, goodwill, and reputation. We exclude human resources from this policy about assets as we have found that boards normally choose to devote a separate Executive Limitations policy to that important topic. Of course, a given board might not make either of these choices. As long as policies always flow from the broader toward the narrower, each further defining or narrowing the meaning of the policy above it, how the groupings occur is immaterial.

Again, we do not imply that the example given here would be acceptable to all boards either in content or in depth. We have found that boards typically prefer to be at least as specific as the following example.

> *Policy Category:* Executive Limitations
>
> *Policy Title:* Asset Protection
>
> The CEO shall not cause or allow corporate assets to be unprotected, inadequately maintained, or unnecessarily risked.

This further definition of the broader policy prohibition of imprudence is more detailed and potentially very useful, but like all policies is open to interpretation. If the board is willing to accept any reasonable interpretation the CEO chooses to give these terms, further definition can be left to him or her. A board that deems tighter restrictions are needed might state that the CEO is *not* authorized to:

. . . Allow insurance protection against theft, casualty losses, and liability losses to board members, staff, and the organization itself to be inadequate

. . . Allow inadequately insured employees access to material amounts of funds

. . . Unnecessarily expose the organization, the board, or the staff to claims of liability

. . . Make any purchase for which normally prudent protection has not been given against conflict of interest, any purchase of more than $X without having obtained comparative prices and quality, or any purchase of more than $Y without a stringent method of assuring the balance between long-term quality and cost, and orders shall not be split to avoid these criteria

. . . Allow intellectual property, information, and files to be at risk of loss or significant damage

. . . Receive, process, or disburse funds under controls that are insufficient to meet the board-appointed auditor's standards

. . . Compromise the independence of the board's audit or other external monitoring or advice such as by engaging for management purposes parties already chosen by the board as consultants or advisers

. . . Invest or hold operating capital in insecure instruments including uninsured checking accounts, bonds of less than X rating, or in non-interest-bearing accounts

. . . Endanger the organization's public image, credibility, or ability to accomplish ends

. . . Change the organization's name or substantially alter its identity in the community

. . . Create or purchase any subsidiary organization unless more than X percent is owned by this organization, no staff member has an ownership interest, initial capitalization by this organization is less than $X, and there is no reasonable chance of resultant damage to the reputation of this organization

Unless the board is willing to accept any reasonable CEO interpretation of terms like "inadequate" liability coverage, "material amounts of funds," "substantially alter," and the various other provisions, it must go still further into detail. We have found most boards willing to stop at about the level of detail shown here.

Policy Control of Investment Management

Beyond financial condition, financial planning, and asset protection, some boards wish to have a more detailed Executive Limitations policy about investments. These are boards that have accountability for large amounts of money belonging either to the organization or to other people. While some boards will consider not delegating this matter to the CEO at all (meaning that the board itself must be responsible for the investments), many decide to delegate the handling of investments subject to requirements that forbid the CEO from working without qualified investment advice and a licensed broker.

Using the approach made possible by its Executive Limitations policies, the board will have already made the overarching policy prohibiting decisions, actions, and conditions that are unethical or imprudent. Now, parallel to the instances described above, the board must determine whether or not it would accept any reasonable interpretation made by the CEO of the terms *imprudent* or *unethical* as these terms relate to investments.

What follows are two examples of further definitions of *imprudent* regarding the handling of investments. We do not imply that these examples would be acceptable to or deemed sufficient by all boards.

> *Policy Category:* Executive Limitations
>
> *Policy Title:* Investments
>
> The CEO will not cause or allow investment strategies or decisions that pursue a high rate of return at the expense of safety and liquidity.

or

> The CEO will not cause or allow an investment strategy to deviate from a risk-averse orientation that emphasizes current income at the expense of total return.

Either of these examples would outline the broad requirement for caution with investment strategies, but both are stated at a level that lacks the specificity many boards require. That is, the range of reasonable interpretation is still too broad for them. Accordingly, what follows are examples of further definitions a board might add to the broader prohibition, saying that the CEO shall not allow:

> . . . Purchases of foreign investments where principal and interest are paid in other than U.S. dollars
>
> . . . Purchases of fixed-income instruments that are not readily marketable
>
> . . . Expenditures of more than $X on the securities of any one corporate issuer
>
> . . . An undiversified portfolio or diversification that deviates from an asset allocation heavily dominated by fixed-income securities

... Purchases of short-term investments that are not rated at least P-1 by Moody's or Standard and Poor's

... The use of brokerage houses not licensed by the National Association of Securities Dealers

For large pension funds or similar organizations, even more specific investment policies have been developed in the Policy Governance manner, enabling board members to be competent stewards without pretending to duplicate the skills of investment professionals.

Boundary-Setting Works for Financial Governance

In our discussion of governing financial management, we have emphasized the need for the board to clarify its values with respect to financial condition and activities, financial planning, asset protection, and investments using the Policy Governance method of boundary-setting and descending-level policies. Clear board values about those decisions and activities deemed unacceptable allow the CEO to understand the range of his or her authority to make decisions in these areas. The unfamiliar practice of negative wording pays off in that boundaries of acceptable performance are established with minimal interference in the CEO's exercise of judgment in the rough and tumble of organizational life. It aids in the board's governance commitment to control all it must, rather than all it can.

So if you are a board member with financial skills, help your colleagues understand sources of risk and considerations to keep in mind when setting criteria about them. Always remember that your proper role is to inform board values, not substitute for them.

You have seen that the board's policies protecting its financial stewardship are statements of board values, less about numbers than about the principles and perspectives that underlie the numbers. Normally, decisions in Policy Governance that are detailed enough to be numerical are framed by policy so they can be made by others. Unlike most traditional boards, Policy Governance boards involve themselves hardly at all in specific numbers or decisions event by event.

The very important issue of financial management, for which the board is accountable, as it is for everything else in the organization, is handled by the board in Policy Governance as any other operational means issue. The board ensures that it has the information it needs, obtained from any qualified source, to enable it to set out its Executive Limitations policies, then delegates the matter to the CEO. Then it rigorously monitors on a schedule of its choosing to ensure that performance is in keeping with its requirements.

Conclusion

This Guide addressed the part of organizational functioning about which many boards worry most: finances. We explained how Policy Governance boards control financial management through policies that, when carefully monitored, allow the board to establish real and sufficient control over the finances of the organization.

About the Authors

John Carver is internationally known as the creator of the breakthrough in board leadership called the Policy Governance model and is the best-selling author of *Boards That Make a Difference* (1990, 1997, 2006). He is co-editor (with his wife, Miriam Carver) of the bimonthly periodical *Board Leadership*, author of over 180 articles published in nine countries, and author or co-author of six books. For over thirty years, he has worked internationally with governing boards, his principal practice being in the United States and Canada. Dr. Carver is an editorial review board member of *Corporate Governance: An International Review*, adjunct professor in the University of Georgia Institute for Nonprofit Organizations, and formerly adjunct professor in York University's Schulich School of Business.

Miriam Carver is a Policy Governance author and consultant. She has authored or co-authored over forty articles on the Policy Governance model and co-authored three books, including *Reinventing Your Board* and *The Board Member's Playbook*. She has worked with the boards of nonprofit, corporate, governmental, and cooperative organizations on four continents. Ms. Carver is the co-editor of the bimonthly periodical *Board Leadership* and, with John Carver, trains consultants in the theory and implementation of Policy Governance in the Policy Governance Academy.

John Carver can be reached at P. O. Box 13007, Atlanta, Georgia 30324-0007. Phone 404-728-9444; email johncarver@carvergover nance.com.

Miriam Carver can be reached at P. O. Box 13849, Atlanta, Georgia 30324-0849. Phone 404-728-0091; email miriamcarver@carver governance.com.

Notes

Printed and bound by CPI Group (UK) Ltd, Croydon, CR0 4YY